NATIONAL GEOGRAPHIC
Reach
INTO PHONICS

FOUNDATIONS

NATIONAL GEOGRAPHIC LEARNING | CENGAGE Learning

Acknowledgments
Grateful acknowledgment is given to the authors, artists, photographers, museums, publishers, and agents for permission to reprint copyrighted material. Every effort has been made to secure the appropriate permission. If any omissions have been made or if corrections are required, please contact the Publisher.

Photography
Cover: ©Edoardo Mazzucco/500px Prime

For product information and technology assistance, contact us at
Customer & Sales Support, 888-915-3276

For permission to use material from this text or product, submit all requests online at
www.cengage.com/permissions

Further permissions questions can be emailed to
permissionrequest@cengage.com

National Geographic Learning | Cengage Learning
1 Lower Ragsdale Drive
Building 1, Suite 200
Monterey, CA 93940

Cengage Learning is a leading provider of customized learning solutions with office locations around the globe, including Singapore, the United Kingdom, Australia, Mexico, Brazil, and Japan. Locate your local office at **www.cengage.com/global**.

Cengage Learning products are represented in Canada by Nelson Education, Ltd.

Visit National Geographic Learning online at **NGL.Cengage.com**
Visit our corporate website at **www.cengage.com**

Printed in the USA
Quad/Graphics

ISBN: 978-13056-51821

Printed in the United States of America
17 18 19 20 21 22 23 24
13 12 11 10 9 8 7 6 5 4 3

Contents

Sound-Spelling: *Mm*

Mmm

Mmm!

Mmm!

Mmm!

1

Mmm!

Mmm mmm!

Mmm!

Mmm!

Sound-Spelling: *Ss*

High Frequency Word

my

WORD COUNT: N/A

My Hat

Mmm?

Mmm!

My hat

2

Ss! Ss! Ss!

7

A hat

4

5

Sound-Spelling: *Tt*

Tap, Tap

WORD COUNT: N/A

Mm!

Tt! Tt!

Mm!

Ss, Ss, Ss, Ss!

Mm! Mm! Mm!

Tt! Tt!

Sound-Spelling: *Pp*

Tag!

8

WORD COUNT: N/A

1

Sss...

Psss!

6

3

7

Psss!

Psss! Psss! Ss!

Psss!

Sound-Spelling: *Cc*

Cc

High Frequency Word

I

I See

8

1

I see a 🐈 !
cat

My 🧢 !
cap

6

3

I see a 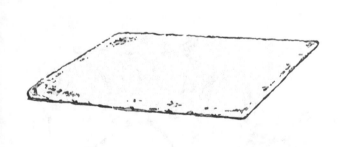.
cap

My !
cat

I see a .
mat

My !
mat

Sound-Spelling: Short *a*

at	cap	mat
pat	Sam	

High Frequency Word

look

Pat Sam

8

WORD COUNT: 13

1

Look at Sam.

A cap

6

3

Sam

Pat Sam. Pat, pat, pat.

2

7

A mat

4

5

Sound-Spelling: *Nn*

can   Nan   nap

High Frequency Word

this

8

WORD COUNT: 20

The Nap

1

Look at this!

6

Cat can nap.

3

Pam can nap.

Look at Nan!

This can nap.

Can Nan nap?

Sound-Spelling: *Hh*
hat

High Frequency Word
is

WORD COUNT: 28

Tap the Hat

1

tap tap tap

6

This is Nan.

3

This is a hat.

Nan can nap, nap, nap.

Nan can tap the hat.

Nan can tap, tap, tap.

Sound-Spelling: *Rr*
ran

High Frequency Word
like

8

WORD COUNT: 25

Pat Ran

1

Pat sat like this.

6

Nan ran at Pat.

3

Look at Nan.

Pat sat, sat, sat!

Nan ran, ran, ran.

Pat ran, ran, ran.

Sound-Spelling: Short *i*

in   nip

High Frequency Word

and

WORD COUNT: 24

© National Geographic Learning, a part of Cengage Learning, Inc.

Nip! Nip!

Mam is in.

Sam can nip at Pat.

Pat is in.

2

Nip! Nip! Nip!

7

Sam is in.

4

Sam can nip and nip.

5

20

Sound-Spelling: *Ff*
fit

High Frequency Word
for

Tip It In

8

WORD COUNT: 25

© National Geographic Learning, a part of Cengage Learning, Inc.

1

Tip it in.

Tip it in for him.

6

3

Tip it in.

I can fit!

Tip it in the pan.

It can fit.

Sound-Spelling: *Gg*
Tag

High Frequency Word
here

WORD COUNT: 22

Tag Can Hit

Can Tag hit it?

Tag can hit.

This is Tag.

2

Tag hit it!

7

Hit, Tag, hit!

4

Here it is!

5

Sound-Spelling: *Bb*

bag   bam   big
bin

High Frequency Word

go

WORD COUNT: 24

Pig Can Go

BAM!

The bin can sit.

The hat can sit.

Look at Pig go!

2

7

The big bag can sit.

Pig can sit.

4

5

Sound-Spelling: Short _o_

Bob   bop   got

hop

High Frequency Word

you

WORD COUNT: 26

Bob Can Hop

Bob can! Hop, hop!

Bob got a pan.

Bob got a can.

Bop, bop!

Bob can tap, tap, tap.

Can you hop and bop?

Sound-Spelling: *Ll*

Gil   lab   lit

High Frequency Word

what

8

WORD COUNT: 25

The Lab

1

Gil can tip it in.

6

Gil is in a lab.

3

What is Gil in?

Look at it!

Dad lit it.

It got hot.

Sound-Spelling: *Dd*

Dad	did	do
mad	sad	Tod

High Frequency Words

do   to

Dad and Tod

WORD COUNT: 31

© National Geographic Learning, a part of Cengage Learning, Inc.

Look at Tod pat Dad.

Dad got mad at Tod.

Dad got mad.

2

Look at Dad pat Tod.

7

"What did you do to
it, Tod?"

4

Tod got sad.

5

Sound-Spelling: *Vv*

Van

High Frequency Words

me   we

The Van

WORD COUNT: 31

"We can hop in!"

Cat can hop in.

Pam can fit in the van.

Pam can not fit in the van!

"We can hop in!"

"Can it fit me?"

Sound-Spelling: Short *e*

fed   get   Mel
Ted

High Frequency Words

have

8   WORD COUNT: 32

Ted and Mel

1

Ted and Mel tip it!

6

Mel can get fed.

3

Ted can get fed.

Ted and Mel can get ham *and* this!

Ted can have ham.

Mel can have this.

Sound-Spelling: *Jj*

Jen   jog

High Frequency Words

he   she

Jog to the Top

WORD COUNT: 32

Don can jog, jog, jog.

Jen can jog.

Don can jog.

Don and Jen jog to the top!

He and she get set.

Jen can jog, jog, jog.

Sound-Spelling: *Ww*

Wes   wet   with

High Frequency Word

come   with

8

WORD COUNT: 28

Wes

1

"Get in, Wes!"

6

"Wes!" Wes ran and ran.

3

"Come with me, Wes."

2

"Wes!" Wes got in.
Sam got wet!

"Come with me, Wes."

4

"Wes!" Wes got wet.

5

Sound-Spelling: *Kk*

Ken   kid   Kim

High Frequency Words

good   they

8

WORD COUNT: 28

The Kid

1

Ken and Kim
ram, ram, ram.

6

Ken can hop, hop, hop.

3

Ken is a good kid.

2

They nap, nap, nap.

7

Ken met Kim.

4

Ken can ram.

5

Sound-Spelling: Short *u*

bug	hum	mud
run	up	yum

High Frequency Word

are

8

WORD COUNT: 32

Hum, Bug, Hum

1

Dig mud, bug. Dig, dig!

6

Run, bug. Run, run!

3

Hum, bug. Hum, hum!

2

Sip, bug. They are good! Yum, yum!

7

Hop up, bug. Hop, hop!

4

Jog, bug. Jog, jog!

5

Sound-Spelling: *Yy*

yak   yes   Yin
yip

High Frequency Words

from   no

8

WORD COUNT: 35

A Yak

1

Yin can ram.

6

Can Yin nip?
Yes, Yin can nip.

3

Yin is a yak.

Pup can run from Yin.
Run, Pup, run!

Pup can yip.

Can Yin yip?
No, Yin can not yip.

Sound-Spelling: *Zz*

zag   zig

High Frequency Word

some   want

8

WORD COUNT: 36

Zig Zig Pig

1

But Pig *can* zig.

6

Dad can zig some.
Zig, zig.

3

Dad and Pig want
to zig zag in the pen.

Zig, zig, zig!

Dad can zag some.
Zag, zag.

Pig can not zag!

Sound-Spelling: *Ququ*
quit   quiz

Sound-Spelling: *Xx*
fix   mix

High Frequency Word
little   play

8   WORD COUNT: 49

In the Mix

1

Play this quiz:
What can Sal do?

6

Pam can fix it.
Pam can not quit.

3

Sam can rub.
Sam can not quit.

2

Sal can get in the mix!

7

Pat got a little wet.
Pat can get a rag.

4

Cat can nip and tug.
Nip, nip, tug!

5

Sound-Spelling: Long *a*

ape	cape	Gabe
game	gate	lake
wave		

High Frequency Words

find	give	that
there		

Gabe Can Play

8   WORD COUNT: 40

© National Geographic Learning, a part of Cengage Learning, Inc.

1

Gabe can get to that lake there.

6

Gabe can find an ape cape.

3

Gabe, an ape, can play a game.

2

Gabe can run in the gate!
Give Gabe an ape wave!

7

Gabe can run.

4

Run, Gabe, run!

5

Sound-Spelling: Long *i*

fine	five	kite
line	Mike	rise
time		

High Frequency Words

how	now

© National Geographic Learning, a part of Cengage Learning, Inc.

8

WORD COUNT: 40

The Kite

1

Mike can tug the line.

6

Mike can take the line.
Mike can run.

3

✂

How can Mike make a
kite rise?

2

Now, it is five. Mike had
a fine time!

7

Mike can let it rise.

4

It can rise up, up, up!

5

Sound-Spelling: Long *o*

home   rope

High Frequency Words

put   said

8

WORD COUNT: 44

The Rope

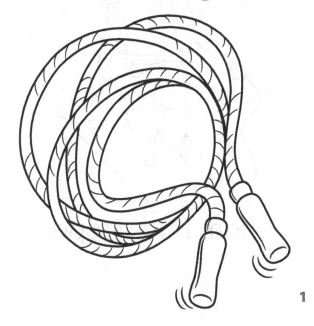

1

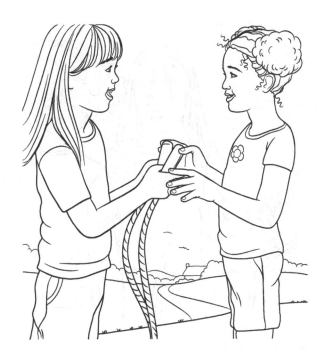

"Put it here," Meg said.
"Hop in, Pam."

6

Jane and Meg did not.

3

Pam had a rope.

"Hop in! Hop in the pot! Hop in! The pot is not hot!"

Meg said she had a rope at home.

Meg got it.

Sound-Spelling: Long _u_

cute   dune   Luke
lute   mule   tube
tune

High Frequency Words

all   one

8

WORD COUNT: 36

© National Geographic Learning, a part of Cengage Learning, Inc.

A Cute Tune

1

"Can Mule make a cute
tune?"

6   "Yes, Luke, I can!"

"Hum on the dune,
Luke."

3

"Hum a cute tune, Luke!"

2

"We *all* can make it!"

"Use one tube, Luke."

"Use one lute, Luke."

Sound-Spelling: Long _e_

Eve   Pete   Zeke

High Frequency Words

your   who

© National Geographic Learning, a part of Cengage Learning, Inc.

WORD COUNT: 41

Pete, Eve, and Zeke

"Look, Pete. Look, Zeke.
My mom got in!"

Pete met Zeke.

Pete met Eve.

Pete, Eve, and Zeke bite,
bite, bite. Yum, yum, yum!

"Eve, did your
mom get in yet?"
"Not yet."

"Who is your mom?"